Whales and Dolphins for Kids
Oceans of The World in Color

Dolphins and whales all belong to a group of marine animals known as cetaceans. Cetaceans are warm-blooded, breathe air, and give birth to living offspring and nurse their young.

Whales are the
largest animals
that have ever
lived on earth
and are the
largest animals
that live in
the ocean.

There are
two types of
whales, Baleen
Whales and
Toothed Whales.
Baleen whales
use a plate of
comb-like fibre
called baleen
to filter small
crustaceans and
other creatures
from the water.

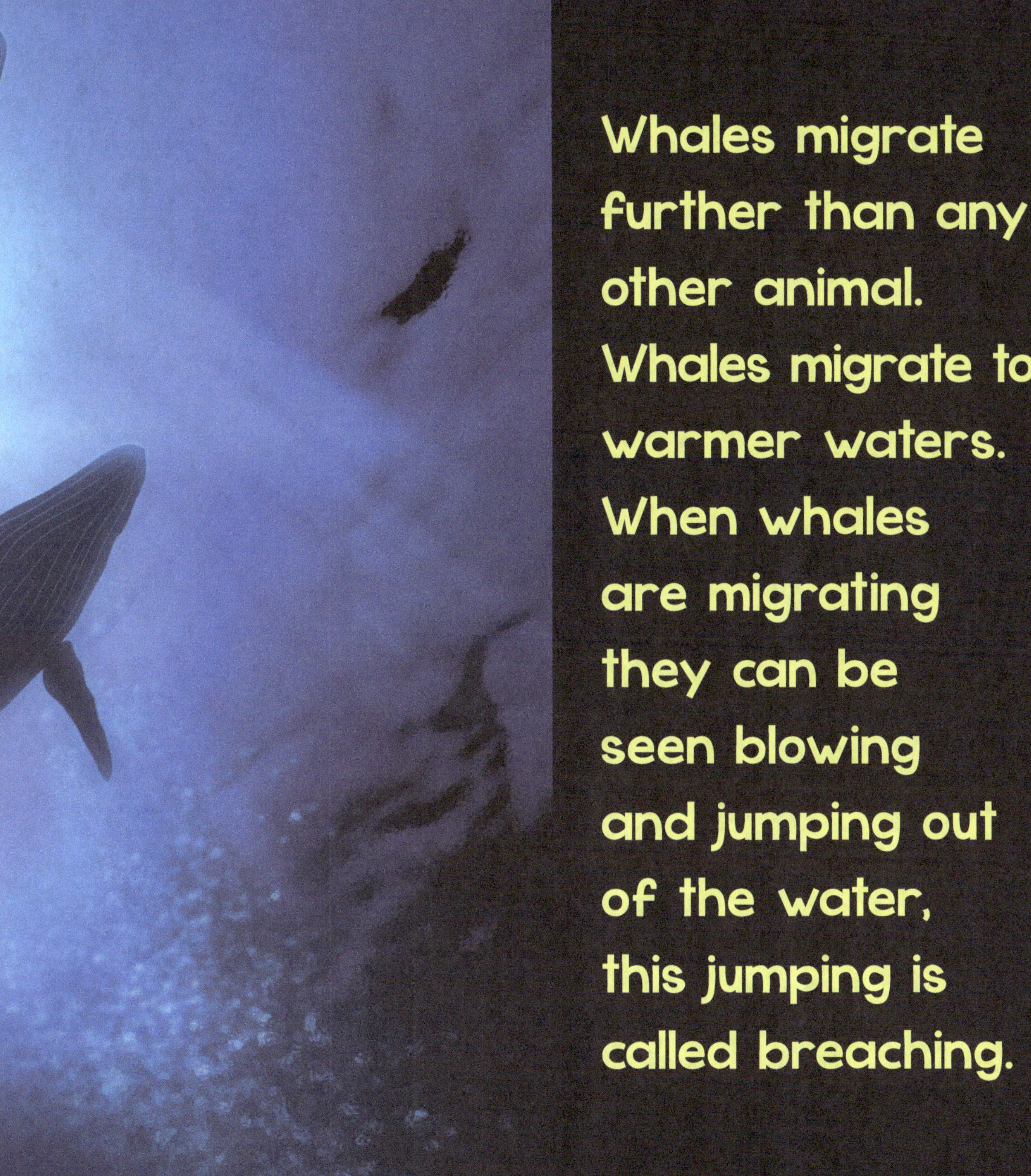

Whales migrate further than any other animal. Whales migrate to warmer waters. When whales are migrating they can be seen blowing and jumping out of the water, this jumping is called breaching.

Whales are the loudest animals in the world. The sounds they make are called "Whale Song." These underwater sounds can travel great distances.

Dolphins live in schools or pods formed by 10 to 12 individuals. Female dolphins are called cows, males are called bulls and young dolphins are called calves.

Compared to
other animals,
dolphins are
believed to be
very intelligent.
Dolphins
communicate
with each other
by clicking,
whistling and
other sounds.

The Killer Whale also known as Orca is a type of dolphin. The killer whale is also the biggest known dolphin.